THE RISE AND FALL OF SAXON
TRANSYLVANIA

By Catalin Gruia

2014

37-Minutes Publishing

First Printing, July 2014

Cover design by Tudor Smalenic

On the cover: **Building *Hermannstadt*.** Saxons came, worked, and built in Transylvania a civilization that reached its peak in the 16th century. Illustration by Radu Oltean.

Translated by Anca Barbulescu

ALSO BY CATALIN GRUIA

Romania Explained To My Friends Abroad

Why We Love Vienna

Thailand With A Baby Stroller

ISBN 13: 9781492354970

CONTENTS

PREFACE

Underdeveloped country seeking investors – this was the slogan of Eastern Europe after the fall of Communism. Like flowers competing for pollinators, its states outdid each other in advertising economic privileges and legislative facilities to attract western investors.

The different governments that took turns in the last 15 years in the Victoria Palace in Bucharest did not bother to go beyond mere declarations of good intentions; but, while TV channels broadcast their formal speeches, the exodus was underway for the most enterprising part of the population, the only one related to the West: Transylvania's German guests.

Eight hundred years earlier, the first Magyar kings wanted to develop a newly conquered land. They, too, needed western human capital, which they attracted with the most generous set of privileges of their time. Saxons came, worked, and built in Transylvania a civilization that reached its peak in the 16th century. For them, prosperity went hand in hand with autonomy. Starting with the 19th century, when history took a nationalist turn, the misfortunes of Saxons came one after the other, culminating in deportations to Siberia, confiscation of property, Communist nationalism and post-revolutionary chaos. Today, they are an endangered people.

Of those left in Transylvania, most are old people who want to die in their homeland. The rest have returned to the West, in search of the same thing that had brought their ancestors to Romania: freedom and economic prosperity.

MEET THE BIRTHLERS

Before we begin, let me introduce you to one of the last German families left in the once-Saxon Reghin (Sächsisch-Regen)

All the Birthlers had gathered in the kitchen. There was a strong smell of cheese. The father, the imposing Herr Alexandru Adalbert Birthler, was passing large pieces of unsalted, fresh cheese through a tiny grinder and merrily nibbling on the crumbs. Frau Lidia-Elena Birthler was commenting the news of the day in righteous horror: some wrongdoers from Glodeni village had vandalized the benches placed on the Mures riverbank by their son Klaus and other volunteers in the "Fata de Mures" (Mures's Face) Association. The father did most of the talking, about how life sometimes knocks you upside the head and how the unfounded optimism of "ignorant children" can be a trap. The children were present, across the table: Klaus Birthler and Georgiana Branea, architects in their 30s, founders of the Fata de Mures Association.

It's been three years since they started to dedicate their weekends to specific activities on the Mures bank, through which they seek to raise awareness of the values of the area among the locals. Georgiana's black eyes were smoldering: "Don't they understand we're doing all this for them?!" After a while, shy, fair-skinned Klaus whispered: "Maybe it was our fault after all, maybe we didn't get the point across."

The Birthlers are one of the ten or twelve families of Germans left in the once-Saxon Reghin (Sächsisch-Regen). Our discussion gradually turns to history. (The Saxons are probably the world's most history-obsessed people: they wrote over 6,000 works on their history and that of Transylvania – in relation to a population that, at its demographic peak, in the period between the two world wars, had 200,000 members.) The Birthlers were speaking Romanian, out of consideration towards me, since I don't speak German. Only Klaus sometimes dotted the conversation with German words, giving the cue to his father who continued it, still turning the grinder handle. This was the end of my journey.

But let me start with the beginning: For nearly two years, I traded Bucharest for a country cabin in Mures. Throughout this time, taking advantage of my travels in the footsteps of the Saxons, I discovered in Transylvania a foreign country. Attempting to reconstruct the final, Transylvanian leg of the journey of the first German colonists, I set out from Alba Iulia (Karlsburg) to Sibiu (Hermannstadt), still uncertain as to what pushed these people forth.

Part 1: The Colonization

THE PROMISED LAND

Like managers with vacancies in the organizational chart, the first Hungarian kings invited guests from the west to develop a Transylvania that was in the process of being conquered.

What made German peasant Hezelo from Markstein (considered to be the first Saxon mentioned by name) sell all his possessions to the Klosterrath monastery in 1148 and leave for Hungary, an unknown land at the edge of the civilized world? Knights participating in the second crusade crossed Hungary in 1147, on their way to Palestine. One of them, chronicler Otto von Freising, described it as the land of opportunity. And still…

Starting from the 11th century, the Holy Roman Empire – particularly its western part, the Netherlands and Flanders of today –

was the leading power in Europe. Technological innovations in agriculture, crafts and mining had brought about an economic boom. The seventy towns in the area between the Rhine and Elbe became three thousand in the 13th century. The population doubled, reaching about twelve million. Due to the new agricultural methods, it took fewer farmers to work the fields. With the economy, the noblemen's claims grew, too. Craftsmen, subject to feudal lords, were burdened by taxes. Their yearning for land and freedom fueled the German migration towards the East. It began in the heart of the country, with deforestations and drainage, and kept spreading to Bohemia, Poland, Lithuania, Moravia, Slovenia, Hungary or Transylvania. Most emigrants were poor peasants, lesser, ruined nobles and their subject craftsmen.

Just as a manager with vacant positions in the organization chart contracts a recruiting company to find the right people, rulers who wanted to colonize a land used the services of a professional "locator". He would travel along selected routes, with summoning documents bearing the rights promised to colonists in the destination territory; on his way back, he would lead the group to the assigned land and sometimes – if he was wealthy enough to support the colony's finances in the first years (as a loan) – become the administrator of the future settlement. The feudal lord granted him a number of plots of land and economic privileges. Although there were several waves of immigration to Transylvania over more than two centuries, the colonization was always planned. The colonists reached Hungary following the Danube. Then they crossed the Tisa River. Those who went upstream along the Mures were assigned lands from the ruler's property, in southern Transylvania, on a strip from Orastie to Baraolt, limited to the north by the rivers Tarnava Mare and Tarnava Mica; those who went up the Somes River reached the Bistrita (Bistritz) area, where most Saxon villages would become vassals to the secular or clerical nobility. According to historian Thomas Nagler, "the Episcopal polity in Alba Iulia and – starting in the second half of the 12th century – the one in Sibiu may have acted as receiving centers. Groups were probably taken over at the border and led to the place they were going to colonize; the chiefs ("greavi", chosen from among the colonists, or clerics, with whom the colonization conditions would also have been negotiated) must have covered the route between their homeland and Transylvania several times."

*

THE MAGYARS TERRORIZED THE WEST for over half a century. Their looting forays seemed unstoppable until 955, when Holy Roman Emperor Otto the Great crushed them in the battle of Lechfeld. The Hungarians abandoned their preying expeditions and formed a state, taking after their vanquishers. They turned their expansion to the south-west, to the Adriatic Sea, and to the east, where Transylvania loomed as a natural fortress, with the Carpathian Mountains as walls.

They conquered it between the 10th and 12th centuries, gradually pushing their frontier eastwards. The new "crown lands" left by the border-dwelling Szekelys, who moved along with the frontier, had to be exploited. Hungarian kings invited "guests" from the west to settle on the lands inhabited by conquered Romanians, Cumans, Pecheneg and Slavs and to develop them. They were promised an enclave free from the domination of nobility and from vassalage, subject only to the king. All countries in Central and Eastern Europe were competing for German colonists. Hungary, which lay furthest into the unknown, raised the stakes by offering the most extensive privileges of its time: personal freedom, land property that could be passed on as inheritance, the right to change lots, local administration and jurisdiction, Church autonomy and calculable taxes.

These privileges would be recorded in writing in 1224 by king Andrew II. But the champion of Transylvanian colonization was his grandfather, king Géza II (1141-1162), who succeeded in attracting Flemish, German and Walloon "guests". The Magyar chancellery called them Saxons – a name having nothing to do with their land of origin, but rather with a legal statute.

"In medieval Hungary, Saxons were the holders of privileges which had initially been granted to miners in Saxony, thanks to their rare skill," says historian Konrad Gundisch.

*

I TRAVELED FROM BRASOV TO TARGU MURES and back again about twenty times before I learned to see it. From the car speeding on the highway, the silhouette of the ruined fortress in Feldioara, barely outlined on a hilltop, appears as a *mirage* wrapped in the dark fog rising from the waters of the Olt River. I made a habit of stopping by the village for a visit to the fortress. Lately, it's actually become crowded, ever since construction began at a large sewage treatment plant at the foot of the hill.

The first Saxon colonists in Feldioara have been unearthed from the small square between the rectory and the Evangelical Church. Local tradition has it that they entered the Tara Barsei region from Rupea, the settlement over the hill, fraying a path with their axes through the Bogata forest. The German name of Feldioara (meaning "earth fortress" in Hungarian) is Marienburg – Virgin Mary's Fortress – after the patron saint of the order of Teutonic knights brought to Tara Barsei around 1211 to defend the southern reaches of the Hungarian kingdom.

Archaeologist Adrian Ionita and his team studied 127 tombs here. The dead were wrapped in gauze and laid, without a coffin, in holes with steps leading down, dug in the shape and size of the human body, with a niche for the head. Here lie two or three generations – from the last years of reign of king Géza II to the coming of the Teutonic order."Analogies with cemeteries in western Europe and Transylvania – areas of Saxon colonization – show that the necropolis in Feldioara belonged to the first wave of German colonists come to Transylvania around the mid-12th century" says Ionita. "Here they formed an autarchic, egalitarian community."

*

SAXONS BROUGHT THE HABIT OF PLANNED settlements to Transylvania. The Flemish-type village became widespread, with homesteads lined up on two rows along one street or square. According to architect Hermann Fabini, "ever since these settlements were founded, there was a tendency to reduce the distance between homesteads as much as possible, for joint, effective action against outside dangers." Each settler got an equal share of the field – split into three areas (for crop rotation over a three-year cycle). Villages were small, around 25 families. Their population rarely exceeded 100. One "sesie" (lot) had as much as 42 acres. Wheat, oats, barley and rye were grown. Forests, meadows and waters were used jointly.

"The Saxons, a people of resolute, steady and unhurried will, chose the land where they would raise their houses and dig their graves based on deeply pondered criteria; they cautiously tasted the water, weighed the light and carefully measured the thickness of the topsoil; they were wary of exceedingly steep heights and tested the direction of the winds with flags and nostrils," wrote philosopher Lucian Blaga in *The Trilogy of Culture*.

In troubled times, in a foreign country at the edge of the world, Saxons learned to live in their communities much like bees in their hives. Individual freedom was sacrificed to the interests of the group of neighbors, that ruled almost all aspects of life and death, of work and play, of rest and faith. Any deviation – as little as swearing, expressing a superstition, lying, drinking or poor hygiene – was punished. Coming from lands with an advanced agriculture, Saxons brought to Transylvania the seeds of economic development. They introduced three-year crop rotation, lot measurement, cereal cultivation, the plow beam with mobile crosspiece, water and windmills etc. The new, more efficient tools accelerated deforestation, the expansion of arable land and increased production. Animals, water and wind power came to the aid of human labor. The 159 mills mentioned in 14th-century documents reflect the improved cereal yield.

Archeological discoveries illustrate the development of crafts and trade. The agricultural progress and strict specialization of crafts enhanced each other. Trade became a profitable occupation, stimulated by the Saxons' right to hold tax-free fairs and travel with their goods without paying customs.

*

IT SEEMED THAT NOTHING COULD STAND in the way of the Mongols, united under Genghis Khan. They conquered China (starting 1211) and the Russian principalities of Kiev and Halych (1223), then they fell upon Europe (1241). The Hungarian army was obliterated at Mohi, the Magyar kingdom fell into ruin, and one quarter of the population was massacred. The campaign was abandoned when news came of the death of great Khan Ögedei, in 1242. Batu Khan returned home, to the heart of Asia, to defend his right to the throne. After this unprecedented invasion, described in Carmen Miserabile by Church official Rogerius from Oradea, many names of settlements, from Rodnei Pass to Oradea, from Tara Barsei to Alba Iulia, disappear from the records.

After 1241, colonization began again, supported by king Béla IV, to repopulate deserted areas. Decades and centuries followed, each with its own share of pillage by Tatars, Turks, Wallachians, Magyars, Austrians or mercenary armies; but the Saxon civilization in Transylvania reinvented itself, sheltered by sturdy walls, in towns (such as Sibiu, Brasov, Cluj, Bistrita,

Sighisoara, Medias etc.) and in over 250 villages with fortified churches. According to historian Thomas Nagler, in the 13th century, through inspired regional management policies, the Magyars had recovered the handicap that separated them from the West: they were a European kingdom with a population of two million, an ethnic melting pot. The first results had been visible for a century: in 1186, king Béla III (1172-1196) asked for the hand of Marie of France, daughter to French king Louis VII. Béla sent the king of France a list of all the income sources of the kingdom. The document, kept in the National Library in Paris, mentions among other things the 15,000 silver marks cashed in each year by the king from his guests. The sum, though probably exaggerated, shows that the Saxons were thriving and that their settlement proved to be a profitable business.

*

ON A TOWER IN SENEREUS, A SAXON VILLAGE in Mures, my area, I found a Latin text which etched itself in my memory: *O quam beata res publica, o quam felix comunitas, quae temporae pacis considerant bella* (How fortunate the country, how happy the community, that in times of peace keeps war in mind).

My wife, Adina, insisted to take me to the villagers' citadel in Rasnov to see this motto made real, in the eagle's nest where she used to play as a child. In the centre of town, she pulled me into an alleyway: let me show you a secret shortcut, through the wood. At the end of the passageway – a narrow path. Ten minutes of climbing irregular steps to the top. The unchiseled stone and brick fortress is surrounded by steep inclines to the south, west, and north.

"When I was little, I used to come here at least once a week. The ruins were covered in grass – no entrance fee and no tourists," my wife said. From the ticket booth, we were taken over by guide Gabriel Guteanu – a slender young man in Bermudas, who looked more like a DJ (I couldn't take my eyes off his plucked eyebrows). A few workers on scaffolding were working on the wall on the eastern side, where we started our tour. The fortress is undergoing renovation; after retrieving it from an Italian licensee who wanted to turn it into a pension, the town administration strives to return it to its former glory.

Mayor Adrian Vestea turned out to have made a lucky bet: the 200,000 ticket buyers (at 2 Euros a ticket) make the Rasnov citadel one of the most visited Romanian destinations in 2011.

Part 2: The Rise

SIBIU, GRAND SQUARE, NO. 8

The Hecht House was the home of a great medieval merchant. It is neither the most beautiful, nor the largest and oldest one in Sibiu. But its metamorphoses and the line of former owners shape the story of the rise of the Transylvanian Saxons.

A walk through *Hermannstadt* (Sibiu) is a trip through both space – the charming labyrinth of narrow streets, communicating courtyards, stone pavements with drains – and time – in a medieval workshop-town, shackled by hundreds of internal regulations. As a foreigner lost in this colorful stone honeycomb crisscrossed by little cobbled streets, I'm looking for the house at no. 8, Piata Mare – the Great Square. Hecht House used to be the home of a great medieval trader. From Elisabethgasse I turn into Brutarilor Street – the Bakers' street, where women used to carry the baskets of leavened dough to the baker's. I pass the Potters' street and get to the Leather Dressers' street. The craftsmen who had workshops here would sell their goods on Tuesdays and Fridays in the Small Square. On the Dyers' street (a continuation of the Leather Dressers' street) there used to be a small stream feeding the craftsmen's workshops. Near the Dyeing workshop, the Leather Dressers' Tower was once painted red.

The corner of Wine Street and Tower Street was the place of the Wine Fair, where Sibiu townsmen would bring their cattle to graze during sieges. In the Huet Square, I circle around the Evangelical church, then enter the upper part of town through an alleyway that used to belong to the shoemakers' guild. The Great Square was where fairs, festivities, trials and executions used to be held – and also where the town's rich men lived. Among them, three foreigners – Oswald Wenzel, Nikolaus de Wagio and Christophorus Italicus of Florence – were commissioned to manage the Hermannstadt Mint in 1456. Their company also obtained rights on the gold and silver mined in Transylvania. No. 9 was the house of Oswald Wenzel, mayor in the 1450s, originally from Bohemia. Next door – Nikolaus de Wagio, a second-generation Sibiu townsman. His father, Italian banker Matthäus Baldi, came to live in Sibiu in the last quarter of the 15th century, managing salt mining in Ocna Sibiului, and administrating the Mint in Sibiu. He had houses in the towns of Abrud and Aiud and, since 1408, this residence in the Great Square.

His closest neighbor was Mint chief Markus, whose house at no. 8 was probably purchased around 1443 by the other member of the trio, Christophorus Italicus of Florence. In the following years, the tide of business took Christophorus to Cluj and then Baia Mare. His son, Paulus Italicus, now owner of the house at no. 8, sold it for 1,000 guilders, on the 1st of June 1472, to Georg Hecht, licensee of the mining exploitation in Baia de Aries and of the Sibiu Mint, owner of all customs points in Transylvania for the trade with Moldova and Walachia. How had Sibiu come to be such a cosmopolitan place, attracting entrepreneurs from everywhere to make excellent business in Transylvania?

*

THE FIRST COLONISTS WHO SETTLED HERE, AROUND THE middle of the 12th century, founded a town twice as big as its neighbors. In less than 100 years, Sibiu became the political and administrative center of the union of colonists, from Orastie to Tinutul Secuiesc. Between 1225 and 1229, due to a land reform ordered by king Carol I Robert, the former Sibiu County was split into seven seats (administrative units): Orastie, Sebes, Miercurea, Cincu, Nocrich, Sighisoara, Rupea, headed by the main seat, Sibiu. Four times, the town moulted, growing out of its walls. In the early 13th century, Sibiu was little more than a bigger village, with fortifications around Huet Square; in the first half of the 14th century, the second ring of walls was built to include the Small Square. In the second half, the walls were extended around the higher part of town, and at the end of the 15th century a fourth enclosure appeared, meant to defend the lower town, up to the neighborhood of the Cibin River. The Mongol invasion in 1241-1242 caused an upheaval in south-eastern Europe, but it created a state of affairs from which Saxon towns benefitted. Hungary was one step away from leaving the game; the Cuman rule to the south of the Carpathians was gone. It was in this power void that the principalities of Tara Romaneasca and Moldova were born. Saxon craftsmen used the two new countries both as sources of raw materials and as markets for their goods (weapons, tools or luxury items). Saxon merchants grew involved in the transit trade connecting Black Sea ports to north-eastern Europe and the lower Danube to the south-west. With the retail system secured, merchants increased their production.

*

FROM THE VERY BEGINNING, HERMANNSTADT was led by people who had money and intended to make even more. The first to get rich were the greavi (small nobility) who had founded settlements – taking their share of the gains from milling, the sale of spirits, slaughterhouses, selling land in town, then long-distance trading. In the following centuries, they were repeatedly replaced at the town hall by a new elite of non-noble entrepreneurs who made fortunes from wholesale and long-distance trading, mining and the administration of various royal sources of income (salt, customs, coin minting). They all proved to be masters at lobbying: they constantly fought to extend and protect trade, making a competition out of collecting economic exemptions and privileges from Hungarian kings. Between 1351 and 1400 only, the Magyar chancellery issued over 40 documents referring exclusively to the situation of Sibiu traders.

*

A TAX LEDGER FROM AROUND 1475, WHEN GEORG HECHT bought the house at no. 8, lists the 896 house owners in town. Taxation was proportional to the taxpayers' wealth. The only people owing more than one silver mark (1 mark = 16 lots = 4 guilders) were 17 patricians – most of them neighbors of Hecht in the Great Square. Members of the city council – formed of four high clerks: the mayor, the vilic (responsible with public buildings and infrastructure) the royal judge and the seat judge, aided by 12 counselors – were chosen from among only 40-50 high-ranking families. Next were retailers and rich craftsmen – about 200 of them, who had made a fortune selling goods out of their workshops.

As early as 1376, Sibiu had 19 guilds with 25 crafts. Hermannstadt worked like a large multi-skilled company, each guild a trade union of sorts for one type of craftsmen who, instead of competing, chose to help each other. In 1480, the town had 920 family heads and 368 tenants – over 6,000 people in all.

*

ON THE 6TH OF FEBRUARY 1486, AT THE REQUEST OF SIBIU mayor Thomas Altenberger, king Matthias Corvinus extended the validity of the Andrean privilege (initially granted by king Andrew II, in 1224, to Saxons in the Sibiu country) over all free Saxon settlements. Thus, the Saxon Universitas was formed – a Parliament of sorts for free Germans in Transylvania.

"The representatives of Saxon seats and districts assembled in Sibiu, usually on Saint Catherine's day, to decide on the correct allocation of tax duties, on prices for goods, on common units of measurement, on guild statutes, on the regulation of all aspects of daily public life, but also on important political issues," says historian Konrad Gundisch. Five years later, merchant Georg Hecht, of Great Square, no. 8, became mayor of Sibiu. It was a prosperous time for the town – and for the house at no. 8, where improvements and renovations were made; its Gothic archways date from that period. The guilds of tailors and shoemakers built new headquarters (on the locations of today's Catholic parish house and Podul Minciunilor, the Bridge of Lies). Construction was finished on the steeple of the parish church of Saint Mary. In 1494, the first pharmacy in town is documented.

During Hecht's mandate, the Turks invaded Transylvania and pillaged the countryside around Sibiu. The mayor, at the head of the army, gave chase and defeated them at Turnu Rosu. Hecht had also led the Saxon cavalry in 1479, in the victory obtained by Pál Kinizsi and István Báthory, ruler of Transylvania, at Campul Painii, against the Turks led by Ali Kodsha. After Georg Hecht's death, in 1496, his son, Johann – Luther's main supporter in Sibiu – inherited by. It held the first Reformationist services (before Brasov citizen Johannes Honterus introduced the Reformation in Transylvania, in 1543).

It was a time of great changes in Transylvania. The Turks defeated Hungary at Mohács (1526). The heart of the country became a pashaluk (1541). Transylvania remained an autonomous principality under Ottoman suzerainty until 1688.

The three privileged groups – Magyar nobility, Saxons and Székelys – ruled the country with equal rights. They chose the prince, they were represented in his councils and had the power of veto against decisions of the Diet that could harm their interests. This is seen as a flourishing time for the Saxon self-administration in the Universitas of the Nation. In 1584, the house at no. 8 was bought by Johann Waida, one of Sibiu's most famous mayors. For the next 237 years, the house remained in the property of the Waida family. They were responsible for many "updates" seen to this day, such as the Renaissance-style gate.

After a long time during which Saxon Comites lived here, in 1821 the Saxon Universitas purchased Hecht House for 20,000 guldens. Repairs amounted to another 12,260 guldens; the floor plan, shape of the roof and aspect of the façade were changed. Currently, there are homes and shops in Hecht House.

Part 3: The Decline

PANDORA'S BOX

The star of the Saxons began to fade in the 18th century, when they failed to obtain the 23rd validation of their privileges. In the era of nationalism, they dealt with a new kind of ruler – the nation state – who was determined to assimilate them at any cost.

I returned to Reghin, where architect Klaus Birthler had put together his family tree. The oldest documented ancestor is Samuel Birthler (1818-1887). It was about the same time that Joseph II of Austria opened Pandora's Box to the Saxons. A kindly, enlightened autocrat, the emperor issued 6,000 edicts and 11,000 new laws through which he attempted, with dismal results, to regulate his subjects' happiness based on rational principles and to turn his hydra of an empire into a modern centralized state. One of these edicts gave Transylvania a new administrative partition into 11 counties, canceling out the autonomies of privileged peoples. The Habsburgs had recognized the Saxon privileges when they took over Transylvania, through the Diploma Leopoldinum (1691).

Though the edict was partly revoked in the year of the emperor's death, the history of Transylvanian Saxons had already taken a new course. Their star started to fade in the 18th century, when they failed to obtain the twenty-third reconfirmation of their privileges. In the age of nationalism, they were faced with a new leader – the national state – determined to assimilate them at any cost. Hungary annexed Transylvania after the rebellion in 1848-1849; Romanians and Saxons stayed faithful to Vienna. Székelys resorted to reprisals: Reghin and several neighboring villages were burned. (This is why Klaus can't find his roots beyond 1848…)

For the Saxons, it was a time of "Hungarification". Hungarian became the official language (1868), guilds were forbidden for being obsolete (1872), the "royal territory" of the Universitas of the Saxon Nation was abolished (in 1876, when the Saxons lost much of their common assets). Dissatisfaction with the Hungarian government and the customs war between Romania and Austria-Hungary (1886-1893), which plunged Saxon towns into a deep economic crisis, gave rise to a wave of emigration: 10% of the 200,000 Saxons left for the U.S.A. or Romania. Once Transylvania became part of Romania, Hungarification was replaced by

Romanization. In the Greater Romania of 1918, Saxons from Ardeal, together with Swabians from Banat and Germans from the pre-1918 Romanian kingdom, Bucovina and Bessarabia, formed the most numerous Germanic community in south-eastern Europe: 800,000 people. But there was more harm yet to come out of the Box…

During the agricultural reform in 1921, almost 15,000 acres were seized from Saxon citizens and over 18,500 acres from Saxon communes, while the Evangelical Church and the Saxon Universitas lost over half of their lands. Financing for education and church – the two fundamental institutions of the Saxons – was deeply affected. The next blow was the decision made by the Bucharest government to impose a 1:2 rate for the exchange of Hungarian koronas into Romanian lei that melted away all Transylvanians' savings, but hit the Saxons particularly hard, as they were wealthier. Starting 1925, the end-of-school examination was held in Romanian only.

*

THE TRANSITION FROM THE PERIPHERY OF A GREAT EUROPEAN Empire to the center of a Balkan country caught the Saxons unprepared; still, they knew how to reinvent themselves, and their economy had another attempt at a comeback. Two thirds of them were peasants. Half of the almost 38,000 Saxon households owned less than 15 acres of land. After the Unification, the Saxons realized they couldn't face the competition of the farmers to the south of the Carpathians, who produced more abundant crops sold at much lower prices, which covered internal demand and left a surplus to export. On the verge of bankruptcy, the Saxons came up with a new revolution: industrializing agriculture.

They brought from Germany farming machines, selected seeds and breeds, fertilizers, new methods for farming and fighting pests. They reoriented themselves towards more profitable fields: animal farming, industrial plants (soy, sunflower, hop, potatoes), medicinal plants, vegetables and fruit. Education played a key role. Itinerant teachers held conferences in village after village to spread new knowledge and new technologies. In 1929, a school of agriculture was founded in Sibiu – holding short classes in winter. The results were quick to show. In the early 20th century, three quarters of the Saxon communes exploited their lands together. The new, industrialized agriculture – particularly in Sibiu, Tarnava Mare and Brasov – yielded wheat and maize crops more than 100% above the country average. In 1925, agronomist Gheorghe Ionescu-Sisesti summarized the situation as follows: "Saxons are the best agriculture and cattle farmers of all the nationalities of the Romanian provinces united in 1918."

*

ALTHOUGH THEY STOOD FOR ONLY 1.37% OF THE
COUNTRY population, the Saxons' total investment into industry
amounted to about seven billion lei in 1934, one third of the
Romanian state budget; 10% of the money deposited in Romanian
banks was entrusted to the over 40 Saxon banks, of which the
General Savings House in Brasov (1825) is thought to be the first of
its kind in Romania.

In 1943, the Germans had 420 enterprises totaling 22,000
workers (12.3% of the national sum total), that accounted for 27%
of Romania's industrial production. The Saxon press boomed in the
years between the two world wars: Sibiu alone had three such daily
newspapers at the same time, plus other cultural or specialized
publications. Circulation was low (five to six thousand for daily
newspapers), but issues reached the entire European German-
speaking area. Having been a privileged ethnic group until 1867,
Saxons did not take well to becoming a minority constantly thrown
against the ropes first by the Hungarian national state, then by the
Romanian one; "in 1930, they chose to form their own nation,
against the state in which they lived," explains historian Cornelius
R. Zach. Disappointed with the Bucharest government, most Saxons
embraced the Renewal movement, a form of nationalist-socialist
protest. In the beginning, many saw a savior in Hitler. In September
1941, during a sermon, Vicar Friedrich Müller declared the "Heil

Hitler" salute to be tantamount to a prayer. Soon, however, "decision was taken from the hands of the community and reserved for a small leading elite and, later for the Central Office for Ethnic Germans in Berlin. With their proud sense of identity, Saxons were thus degraded to becoming mere instruments," says Zach.

While Germany was riding its wave of glory, Saxons lived well, too. Bishop Viktor Glondys, an adversary of the national-socialist ideology, wrote in his diary in 1941: "No one has dared to stand up against the Renewal Movement, not only because they were afraid that Germany would see them as an adversary of national-socialism, but also because, without this movement, the Saxon people would be deprived of the money from Germany." There were hopeful talks of an autonomous Transylvania under German protectorate. But Hitler had other plans: on August 30th 1940, in Vienna, he decided to split Transylvania between Romania and Hungary. North-western Transylvania and its 34,000 Saxons were annexed by Hungary.

*

STARTING SEPTEMBER 1940, BERLIN APPOINTED YOUNG SAXON Andreas Schmidt as the head of the Ethnic German Group in Romania. He succeeded in spreading Nazism to the majority of Germans in Romania, who had now become a war accessory of the Third Reich. After the invasion of the U.S.S.R., ethnic Germans from Germany's satellite states became a reserve for the German army. 70,000 Romanian Germans joined the SS or the Wehrmacht and contributed to the German war industry. 26,000 of them were Saxon. When Romania turned the weapons against Germany, they were all declared to be defectors. By personal appointment by Hitler, General Arthur Phelps became Transylvania's SS and police chief. One of his orders: taking any measure necessary to save the Germans in Transylvania and Banat. He only succeeded in evacuating the Saxons in Northern Ardeal. Opinion leaders of the southern Saxons opposed his attempts. "Those who stir without reason hurt the heritage of their forefathers and their holy duty towards their children," said, in an interview in September 1944, lawyer Hans Otto Roth, who had become an unofficial leader of the German population in Romania.

In the north, the evacuation followed a careful plan. German officers returned from the eastern front insisted that the Russians would massacre any German they find in their way. General hysteria ensued. On the 17th of September 1944, in Lechinita, Bistrita County, the bells no longer called the 1,100 Saxons to Sunday morning mass. It was the evacuation signal. The convoys left in perfect order, led by German soldiers. The same ritual was repeated everywhere: a short religious service, a common prayer and, at the bell's signal, the start.

Klaus' grandfather, Josef Birthler, a mechanic foreman in Reghin, was one of the 30,000 Saxons evacuated from the town – 95% of the population. The value of the abandoned properties amounted to about 500 million dollars in gold, at the value in 1944.

*

IN THE RASNOV HOUSE THAT USED TO BELONG to his parents, with his ears straining to hear the antique radio the size of an altar, with family photos and badges for icons, the old man is listening to morning mass on a German radio station. His lips are sunken in and surrounded by vertical lines so deep that his mouth looks like a grouchy zipper. But don't be fooled by appearances. If you get to know him, old man Hans (Gagas Johann) becomes a witty guy who, at 93, still "loves girls" and plays some mean drums in Fanfara Tarii Barsei, the area's brass band.

Even while deported to the U.S.S.R., in the Donbass camp, where his peers lived for three years "like cattle," he would dispel the prison mood for a while by playing the drum he had fashioned "out of a preserve tin, a spring and a piece of wire". Old man Hans fought in the Romanian army during the Second World War. He spent eleven months in the first line of the Caucasus front. It made no difference. After the war, both he and his wife were deported to the U.S.S.R. along with 70,000 German ethnics in Romania. 14,000 died due to hard labor and shortages. "Innocent, all of them."

The Saxons evacuated from Northern Ardeal lived through an ordeal of their own, orchestrated by their Romanian fellow countrymen. In the weeks after the 13th of September 1944, when the last German and Hungarian soldiers withdrew from Northern Ardeal, Saxon households were looted by neighboring Gypsies and Romanians, who stole everything they could. In villages like Ghinda, Chirales or Tarpiu, some had taken the habit of moving from one absentee house (a term used by Romanian authorities for the departed Saxons) to the next every few days.

Between October 1944 and the autumn of 1945, the Romanian authorities reinstalled in Northern Ardeal brought 2156 families of Romanian colonists in the towns and villages deserted by Saxons. The agricultural reform on the 23rd of March 1945 took the lands away from German ethnics. One quarter of the evacuees were overtaken by the Red Army on Reich territory and sent back to Transylvania during the summer and autumn of 1945.

Their fear of a Russian massacre turned out to be unfounded. Rudolf Schuller, curator of the Evangelical church in Bistrita, told of colonel Serbakov, the Russian military commander: "He showed none of the hatred towards Germans which Romanians displayed." In some areas, Romanians beat up their neighbors when they returned. According to report no. 635/August 24th 1945 issued by the Gendarmerie of Nasaud County, the mayor in Tarpiu robbed the Saxons who returned to the village. Order no. 7499/May 26th 1945, as issued by the general police headquarters: "…take measures to see that all German citizens departed with the German troops and returning to their homes be arrested and sent to camp."

Unwanted by those who had gotten hold of their fortunes, Saxons were styled as "traitors of their motherland who leeched on the Romanian nation". Ioan Popu, who had only recently been appointed chief of the Nasaud prefecture in June 1945 and who grew to be known as the Saxon Eater, sent a confidential note, no. 8999/July 5th 1945, to the Ministry of Home Affairs, requesting the deportation of the Saxons returned to the Bistrita area and living, at the time, in a camp in another part of the country, "so that they give up any thought that they will ever return to their properties, where we have settled citizens with a right to own the land."

All German ethnics were sent to labor camps as "community service," far from their places of origin. Klaus' grandfather, Josef Birthler, had a different experience. After the evacuation, he only made it to Budapest, where he was badly injured by a grenade. He lay in a hospital, struggling between life and death. He fell in love with the Hungarian pharmacy attendant who looked after him, but in the end the love for the Mures's banks (the family curse, as Birthler senior calls it) was stronger and grandpa Josef returned, later but still during the Saxon persecution. He changed his name to that of his Hungarian grandmother and declared himself Hungarian.

*

THE SITUATION ONLY STARTED TO LIGHTEN IN 1948.
Most labor prisoners were set free. Reparatory measures were
attempted in the 1950s: the survivors returned to their hometowns,
got back their right to vote and attend German schools and were
given back their churches. But more misfortune was waiting in
Pandora's Box. An all-powerful communist state was established in
Romania, with increasing nationalist tendencies after the 1960s. For
Saxons, it meant discrimination, uncertainty, hindrances, prison, and
displacement to the Baragan plain. It was also when the paid Saxon
exodus began. At the height of its economic boom, Federal
Republic of Germany needed labor. Its authorities initiated
protocols with all Eastern European countries with German
minorities. According to Florian Banu, researcher at the National
Council for the Study of Securitate Archives (CNSAS), secret
negotiations between Romania and FRG resulted in over 200,000
German ethnics leaving the country between 1962 and 1989. One
Saxon graduate thus "exported" brought 3,000$ to the country
treasury. One student – 1,500$. After the fall of Ceausescu's
regime, the borders were open and, in only two years (between 1990
and 1992), the huge majority of Germans in Romania (another
160,000) left the county freely.

*

AT THE TOP OF THE ROOFED STAIRWAY at the entrance of the fortified church in the Sarosul pe Tarnava village, I asked the guard how many Saxons still live in the village. "Three families. All of them old people." How does one feel about the turn of the wheel of history for his ancestors, who in the 14th century started to raise here a stone fortress of the Church, meant to last a thousand years?

I was walking through the empty church like a ghost, weighed down by burdening thoughts. The air was heavy with the scent of the black locust tree blooms. Could it have been worse? Certainly! According to historian Ernst Wagner, "Romania does not look so bad if we compare its attitude towards German ethnics to that of other Eastern European countries, such as Poland or Czechoslovakia." The Birthlers signed up for emigration in the '80s. They were written in somewhere near the bottom of the list and never made it out. Around 1992, they did visit their relatives in Germany, but "we wouldn't stay…"

After 1990, with the massive exodus of the Saxons, their houses were given to other locals – Romanian and Gypsy. The Saxons moved to the Diaspora: 200,000 live in Germany, about 20,000 in Austria, 30,000 in the U.S., 8,000 in Canada. Rohtraut Wittstock, chief editor of Allgemeine Deusche Zeitung für Rumänien, estimates that there are only 15,000 Saxons left in

Romania – most of them elderly. And a few idealistic young people like Klaus, who feel connected with this land.

I said goodbye to Klaus on a rainy Saturday, after helping him build a pontoon on Canalul Morii in Reghin. The town's anniversary was coming up the following day and Klaus, ever the optimist and ever in love with the Mures, was preparing boating lessons for the local children. "Have you noticed that most Romanians build their houses facing away from the river? In other countries, having your address next to a body of water is an honor... We must learn to turn our faces back to the Mures."

Part 4: Tourism Today

ROMANIA'S GERMAN HERITAGE

16 Saxon Discoveries in Transylvania

Tombs and moss and grass and ancient slabs and cobbled alleys and centuries-old trees are placed in a flowing, snaking pattern, following the lines of nature, in a terraced cemetery stretching over 4,5 hectares on Sighisoara's highest hill. I had been in the citadel several times before, but I had never climbed up here. The wind was blowing gently, the world seemed enchanted in the Cemetery on the Hill, floating in a dawn-of-the-world kind of peace and quiet. Eager to find out more about this unbelievable place, as soon as I left it I headed straight to a stern-looking lady in front of the Evangelical Church, a couple of steps from the cemetery's iron gate. That's how I learned – from Lenuta Orban, wife of the grounds manager who lives right there, in the Ropemakers' Tower, like in a fairytale house – the history of the biggest and oldest (dating from 1704) Saxon cemetery.

Such random encounters with extraordinary locals are the salt and pepper of successful travels and bring about the most unexpected revelations. Lately I've chanced upon many revelations and random encounters. After 800 years the Saxons returned to the West, seeking the same thing that had brought their ancestors here: liberty and economic prosperity. Their heritage, however, remains and calls us to discover it. For your next Transylvanian escapade, I have asked a few well-informed fellow travelers to recommend to you a Saxon discovery.

HIKES IN THE HEART OF TRANSYLVANIA

Illustrator **Radu Oltean** discovered in 1991 the picturesque charm of hiking from one Saxon village to another, from one valley to the next, over the low, densely forested mountains. Gentle, friendly slopes, woods, crossing fields of corn, alfalfa or potatoes, hills still terraced from the work done on the old abandoned vineyards, deer, storks and short distances between places of interest drew the attention of groups of enthusiasts who, in the last few years, have started to promote trips (on foot or by bike) in the area. Recently, itineraries have been marked and detailed maps have been printed. The Tarnava Mare valley and the Hartibaciu valley draw the boundaries of the biggest forested hill area in Transylvania, which has survived due to the local regulations of the Saxon villages (in the pre-communist decades) and the respect for the communal forest land of each village. The tiny valleys hide beautiful Saxon settlements, visible from afar thanks to the spires of the mediaeval churches, rising like donjons.

RHUBARB JAM FROM HAMBARUL ALIMENTAR

"If you take a tour of Transylvanian fortified churches, you simply have to stop in Saschiz, a Saxon village about 20 kilometres from Sighisoara on road DN13, with a 15th century citadel included on the UNESCO World Heritage list," recommends photographer **Bogdan Croitoru**. "Saschiz also discretely preserves some small secrets that may hide unsuspected joys. In 2009, Prince Charles visited Saschiz for the inauguration of a processing centre for the area's farmers, called Hambarul Alimentar – the Food Barn. This production unit, actually an old, repurposed Saxon barn, is authorized to retail in Romania and abroad, supporting small regional producers who use traditional methods, first trained through a course organized by the Royal Society for Public Health. The Barners sell to tourists, visitors of fairs with traditional products and especially British clients (Royal Family included) jams, pickles, fine blue cheeses, plant-based products, cakes, bread, drinks and oils. One highly sought-after Saxon delicacy is rhubarb jam. Thought to have been brought to Germany from Asia around the half of the 16th century, it is highly likely that rhubarb reached Transylvania thanks to Saxon traders. Rhubarb jam is refreshing, slightly tart. The parts of the plant must be carefully chosen, as the leaves contain toxic oxalic acid; rather than going through the trouble of making it at home, go buy it from a Saxon housewife. It reinvigorates you, it regulates digestion and puts wings where you remembered your shoulder blades to be."

More details at: Tourist Info Center, ADEPT Foundation, str. Principala no. 166, Saschiz, jud. Mures 547510 Romania, phone no.: 40 (0)265 711635

THE ST. MICHAEL CHURCH HILL, CISNADIE

"Exhausted after 20 hours of driving straight from Amsterdam, I parked in Cisnadioara and, with my last sliver of energy, climbed up the hill to the old St. Michael (Sf. Mihail) church," says *National Geographic Netherlands* editor **Pancras Dijk**. "At sunset, I felt as though I had been transported to the 12th century, having found a beautifully restored church that looked like mass was about to start in it, with walls ready to withstand any Ottoman or Tatar threat. Spread all over the plateau, many perfectly round boulders stood witness to the titanic task young men were required to fulfill in order to be recognized as adults: rolling one of these stone balls all the way from the valley to the top. But all these testimonies of the past were silent. There was not a man in sight. It looked like not just the Saxons, but the rest of mankind had deserted this hill, too. Meanwhile, I've travelled high and low in Transylvania in search of its Saxon heritage. On the last day, in the Rucar-Bran area, I drove to Cisnadie to buy a genuine "Cisnadie carpet".I couldn't help myself – I covered the extra few kilometers to visit the church a second time. By some quirk of fate, it was also the time when the sun was setting over the enchanting scenery. I could hardly believe my eyes: this time, the church and the plateau were full of artists, poets, musicians, spectators, both young and old, many of them from Sibiu. The event I was witnessing was called Exodus, but in fact I was quite happy to find that life had returned there. The Exodus had breathed life back into the history of this sacred hill – and it had given it a future, too."

THE SHORTCUT TO THE RASNOV CITADEL

"Just 15 minutes from the historic town center lies the place I love more than any other in Rasnov, the place where I take anyone visiting our country for the first time: the citadel," says **Adina Branciulescu**, coordinator of the *Beau Monde* magazine.

"There are two routes leading to it: the comfortable one, by car, branching off from the road to Poiana Brasov, and the slightly more difficult one, on foot – which I prefer by far. From the centre of Rasnov, you go through the passageway cutting through a Saxon building, the old culture centers, and you find yourself at the edge of the forest. The climb is easy and pleasant, and the view – more and more beautiful as you go. You can see the geometrically aligned streets, bordered by Saxon houses with tile roofs, the Evangelical Church, the Codlea hill, the mountains, forests and neighboring towns. Until recently, I used to come here just for the pleasure of the walk, but in the mean time the citadel itself has become interesting, more spectacular with each passing year. It is renovated, it has guides, souvenir shops and it hosts festivals all year long: Life in the Citadel, the Jousting Tournament of the Citadels, the Mediaeval Festival and the International Historic Film Festival. From there, I would recommend going down the other side of the citadel: At the bottom you will find a hotel with a restaurant and well-tended sports courts – the locals call it Acapulco. Rest for a few minutes, then continue on to the Valea Cetatii cave. It's easy to find, the path there is marked, and if the day is hot the coolness of the cave will be welcome (you absolutely need a warm jacket, though)."

PS: Thanks to the excellent acoustic qualities of the cave, symphonic music concerts take place there on Saturday afternoons (http://pestera-valeacetatii.ro).

PSS.: In 1965, a hotel-restaurant was opened at the foot of the citadel hill, called by locals "Acapulco" because Fun in Acapulco, starring Elvis Presley, had been shown in local cinemas in the same period; in it, the main character dove from a cliff that resembled the one next to the hotel.

TRANSYLVANIAN BRUNCH

"On the last Saturday of each month from April to September, the villages in the Hartibaciu-Tarnava Mare Plateau organize a culinary and cultural event," says **Alina Alexa** of the Association for Ecotourism in Romania (AER). "In summary, each edition shows off the beauties of a village, an orchard, a traditional household, a historic monument or a community. The ingredients come from local households, and the recipes are the result of centuries of multiethnic cohabitation: from cheese specialties and Romanian soups to székelykáposzta and Saxon hanklich." The full program of Transylvanian Brunch is available at http://brunch.dordeduca.ro/.

"After the feast, there's also a helping of culture: a hike, a ride on the rail-cycle draisine, a concert, a crafts workshop and so on, depending on what we find in the villages," says Cristian Cismaru of Reki Travel. "To join the brunches, you have to make a reservation by e-mail to transilvanian.brunch@gal-mh.eu. There have been a lot of people interested lately – once we reach around 150-200 participants (depending on the location) we no longer take reservations, in order to preserve the quality of the event."

THE PROCESSION CROSS AND SAXON TALES

"Go to the museum in the Evangelical Church in Cisnadie to see the procession cross, said to have been carried at the head of the Saxon trail when they came to Transylvania in the 12th century," urges architect **Klaus Birthler** from Reghin. "The hill church in Cisnadioara is a Romanic basilica – the most faithful representation of the style that has been preserved in its original form. The other churches were extended and modified according to the styles of the respective times, based on the Romanic basilica plan. The book *Sächsische Volksmärchen aus Siebenbürgen* (Popular Saxon Tales of Transylvania) by Josef Haltrich (probably influenced by the Grimm brothers, with whom he exchanged letters) include two tales: *The Wonder Tree (Der Wunderbaum)* and *The Swan-Woman (Die Schwanenfrau)*. http://www.siebenbuerger.de is the website of the Transylvanian Saxon community, a great communication and information platform maintained by Saxons who have emigrated. In Germany, Saxons who have left Transylvania meet once a year at Dinkelsbühl, in Bavaria. They form groups named after the Transylvanian villages of their parents, grandparents or great-grandparents."

Woolen socks from Viscri

"It's hidden like a dusty treasure at the end of a bumpy, unpaved road, among tall trees and fields that are either green or white, covered in dandelion fluff," says **Andreea Campeanu**, a stringer for Agence France-Presse. "Viscri could be touristy, but it isn't, because it's far, hard to reach and has every intention to stay that way. Its houses with thick walls painted in vivid colors, lined along the wide, muddy road, are only reachable by brave cars and the horse-drawn wagons of the locals – the few remaining Saxons, a few Romanians and the Gypsies. With the ash-colored fortress at the top of the hill, full of labyrinthine nooks, Viscri, in its simplicity, always offers the joy of discovery. Such as the surprise when, lined up over a big, Saxon-style wooden gate, you find handmade woolen socks, house slippers and small shoulder bags, alone and unguarded, maybe forgotten there by a village woman who ran inside to cook dinner, knowing how rarely buyers pass on her street."

The Saxon mountain shelters

"In 1880, in Sibiu, the *Siebenbürgische Karpatenverein (SKV)* was founded – Romania's first large organization dedicated to nature exploration, research and protection and to tourism in the Carpathians. A National Geographic Society of sorts, only 8 years older. (Right after the establishment of the NGS, collaboration with the SKV was initiated.) The SKV built over 60 mountain shelters in the southern Carpathians, some of which are still standing at Balea, Curmatura, Omu, Suru, Barcaciu, Negoiu etc. In 1945, the communists dissolved the SKV and nationalized the mountain shelters. A few Saxons from Germany re-founded it in 1996," says **Cristian Lascu**, editor-in-chief of *National Geographic Romania*.

SAXON CERAMICS AND BAUMSTRIEZEL

"Buy Saxon vases and plates," advises **Madalina Nan**, tour operator. "Apart from traditional costumes, ceramics are another element that defines the Saxon community in Transylvania. Ceramic vases or mugs with floral motifs, sometimes accompanied by the emblem of their regions of origin, are omnipresent in Saxon houses or churches. Pottery was an art in the Saxon community. The first potters' guilds date back to 1376. They required craftsmen to undergo rigorous training and produce very high quality ceramics of great artistic value. Also, a cultural recommendation: the Saxon equivalent of the delicious kürtôskalács (Saxon breadroll) is leavened dough baked in the hearth, on an open flame, originating in south-eastern Transylvania. The raised dough is gently rolled out, cut into strips and laid in a spiral around wooden rollers. The baumstriezel is then glazed with melted butter and sugar, then left to bake… and the result is a delicious dessert that, much like the Romanian cozonac (yeasted sweet bread), is never absent from any Saxon holiday."

A VILLAGE CALLED BIERTAN

"20 years ago I watched in fascination, on Deutsche Welle TV, a documentary about a centuries-old church, with a mechanism to secrete away riches, and about long-forgotten traditions for making spouses get along again," says travel blogger **Cezar Dumitru**. (http://www.imperatortravel.ro/). "Then, at the end, I was stupefied to find out that special place was in Romania, in an out-of-the-way Saxon village on a secondary road close to Sighisoara. Years later, I discovered that little-used road myself, snaking between fairytale hills to a village called Biertan, or Birthälm, in German. In vineyard country, in the heart of a traditional Saxon village, you are greeted from afar by the famous fortified church, Romania's first monument included in the UNESCO World Heritage list. Biertan lost administrative centre statute to Medias, so it was given the right to host the Saxon episcopate, which remained there for over three centuries – that explains the size of the fortified church in the village. You can get to the Gothic church at the top of the hill by climbing a flight of stairs shaded by a wooden roof much like the one in Sighisoara. The Evangelical church, austere, opposed to Catholic luxuries, is one of Romania's Gothic wonders. But what really makes it stand out is the door to the sacristy, where, behind a complex system made up of no less than 19 locks, created in 1515 by local craftsmen, the Episcopal treasure was kept. Another thing not to miss is the cell in the eastern bastion, where arguing couples who wanted to divorce were *imprisoned* for two weeks, with one plate, one spoon, one mug and one bed. Of all the couples that were subject to the experience, only one still wanted to divorce – the rest made up."

THE EVANGELICAL CHURCH IN HERINA

"Only 16 kilometers away from Bistrita, on the crown of a hill next to Herina village, Romania's best preserved Romanic church rises proudly," says university assistant **Gabriela Cocea**. "The exterior, painted in immaculate white, impresses through the austerity of its lines, through the unfinished symmetry of its two uneven towers (that, on a smaller scale, remind the famous cathedral in Chartres). If you want to go in, ask around for Brighite Budacan, who holds the key; at any rate, it's best to try and visit around noon, when you are most likely to find her in the church, looking after the holy place with the Saxons' ancestral diligence. Once inside, you will notice the interior looks more like an unusual art gallery: the walls and the white columns bear the works of a Transylvanian artist – a different one each year. This year, the church is decorated with the tapestry and embroidery works of artist Zoe Vida Porumb. Don't forget to look for the mural piece preserved to the left of the simple wooden altar, or the stone face on the base of one of the columns. Mass is no longer held in the church, and the Saxon population has gradually left the area, with only five Saxons still living in the village. One of them is our guide – ask and he will tell you, nostalgically, about how Saxon traditions still survive in the maelstrom of a century that threatens the entire rural civilization, regardless of its forebears."

THE COUNTRY HOTEL

"I never forgot the white towers of the Harman citadel, standing stark against the postcard-blue sky, the wooden stairs leading to the old pantries, the shaded walkway from which you can watch, from a laid-back past, the village that looks forever frozen in a Sunday," says **Roxana Farca**, travel writer for LumeaMare.ro.

"It's the kind of peace you only find in Austria or Germany. Close to the citadel I met Marcela Cosnean, who created in her

B&B, The Country Hotel, a home into which you wish you could move for good, as long as the host can stay around too. Marcela is an amazing cook and is not afraid to challenge you with unusual recipes and combinations you've never tried before. Conversations flow merrily, the delicacies on the table vanish in a blink, and the good wine keeps them company. You will enjoy the most restful sleep in the home-sewn linen sheets. We took home with us the memory of the morning sun gliding in through the windows, playing in the colors of the homemade jams, Marcela's energizing laughter in our ears and the white image of the citadel under our eyelids – a place so serene in times that are otherwise undeservedly troubled."

THE APPRENTICE HOUSE

"I was in highschool when the first apprentices came to Sibiu to live in the Apprentice House in Huet Square no. 3," remembers **Ana Benga**, German kindergarten teacher, who studied at the German Pedagogy Highschool in Sibiu.

"Afterwards, apprentices kept coming to Sibiu – particularly young Austrians, Germans and Swiss, less than 25 years old, who must carry out their practice in various places of the world. By custom, they have a few rules to observe: wearing their traditional costume, not communicating with their families, not working for money etc. The minimum duration of their voyage is two or three

years and a day and it must be established before departure. Usually, Sibiu is visited by bricklayer, carpenter and stonemason apprentices who, throughout the years, have worked for the renovation and restoring of many houses in Sibiu. You can recognize them by their compulsory traditional attire, specific to each guild, and you often find them near the Evangelical church that owns the Apprentice House (that is located in the Stairs Tower connecting the upper city to the lower city and has hosted travelling apprentices for centuries). In 2007, the Casa Calfelor (Apprentice House) Association was founded. If you meet any travelling apprentices around town, strike up a conversation (they speak English) and find out about the history and secrets of their craft."
http://www.casacalfelor.eu/ro/despre-noi/

THE CALNIC CITADEL

"Next time you're on European road E60 connecting Sibiu to Sebes, take a short detour to Calnic," says **Razvan Pascu** (www.RazvanPascu.ro), tourism blogger and consultant, "to experience the peace, order and feeling of «normality» exuded by the citadel that, since 1999, is part of the UNESCO World Heritage. Initially, Calnic was the residence of a Transylvanian count, later turned into a fortification for the village. That may be precisely why it was kept so well, while its picturesque quality is due to the locals' care for the citadel. I have rarely seen people repairing windows in citadels (many of them don't even have any left), or video surveillance, or a well-tended, functional chapel that, on top of everything else, welcomes tourists with the sounds of an organ (recorded, it's true, but it's the atmosphere that matters)."

DUPA ZIDURI, IN BRASOV

"Take a romantic walk at sunset on the Dupa Ziduri (Behind the Walls) Alley," says stomatologist **Diana Tret** from Brasov. "On one side you have the forest, on the other the city walls… All you can hear is the rustle of the trees and the gurgle of the Graft/Spurcata stream. The walk will introduce you to the city's outer fortifications: you will pass by the Black Tower (that got its name after it was struck by lightning twice), the White Tower, that was assigned for defense to the pewter and brass workers' guild, and the Graft Bastion, hosting a section of the Brasov County History Museum, with information on the guilds' role in the defense of the city."

PIECES OF HISTORY IN SACELE

"Let yourself be charmed by a break in Sacele, a village with typical Saxon architecture, an old Catholic church (presently a monument), partly renovated, beautifully perched on the top of a hill, many small Orthodox churches scattered throughout the village, and the air of a place outside time," advises journalist **Anca Popescu**. "Wandering on the sloping, narrow streets, past the large, apparently impenetrable gates, you will eventually find an open gate, like an unspoken invitation. There you will find, like in a fairytale, what no one would expect to find behind the gates' old wood: flowers of all shapes and colors, old shady trees, the omnipresent grapevine arch and a fresh lawn. The smiling host will certainly offer you all you need – a good meal, a clean room, a lot of peace and quiet. The forest by the village leads to Bunloc, where you can take the chairlift to take in the scenery; with a bit of luck, you'll see that it's also the favorite takeoff place for paragliders. You could try a "double" with an authorized instructor – I can assure the experience is well worth it!"

FOR THOSE IN LOVE WITH SIEBENBÜRGEN

Are you familiar with Saxon Transylvania? Know some tips about where to eat or stay, or what to do in a town we haven't mentioned here? Whether you are a local or a devoted visitor, we would like you to share them with us (unless you have a business interest in the activity you recommend). Send us your tips at catalin.gruia@gmail.com. Be precise: tell us what you like (for instance, a particular restaurant) and why (your favorite menu item). Include your name, place of residence and what draws you to Transylvania.

Timeline

THE ASCENT AND DESCENT OF A CIVILIZATION

Key dates in the 800 years history of Saxons in Transylvania

1141-1162 – king Géza II invites "guests" from Western Europe to defend and develop the new "king's land" in Transylvania.

1211-1225 – The Teutonic knights are settled in Tara Barsei to secure the southern frontier of the Magyar kingdom.

1224 – The Diploma Andreanum establishes the rights and obligations of German colonists.

1241-1242 – A Mongol mega-invasion devastates south-eastern Europe. Many Saxon settlements are razed to the ground.

1325 – The Saxon rebellion against the ruler of Ardeal is suppressed. The seat constitution is instated.

1395 – First Ottoman attack on Tara Barsei.

1486 – king Matthias Corvinus confirms the unity of Saxons on the lands of the crown (Universitas Saxonum).

1526 – The battle of Mohács; the central part of the Hungarian kingdom becomes a pashaluk.

1541 – The first Saxon secondary school is inaugurated in Brasov. In the early 16th century, each Saxon village had a school.

1542 – The Transylvanian Diet recognizes the suzerainty of the Ottoman Porte.

1542 – Johannes Honterus introduces the Reformation in Brasov and Tara Barsei.

1547 – Ecclesiastic regulations for all Saxons in Ardeal. Saxons become Lutherans.

1595-1606 – Troubled years for Transylvania. Rudolf II of Habsburg wants the Ardeal, recently conquered by Mihai Viteazu, initially in the name of the emperor.

1557-1568 – Religious tolerance in Transylvania.

1572 – Saxons adopt the Augsburg Confession. Biertan becomes the seat of the Evangelical Lutheran bishop.

1583 – Private civil law is introduced for Transylvanian Saxons.

1689 (April) – The great fire in Brasov. Saint Mary's Church becomes the Black Church.

1734 – Lutherans from central Austria are displaced to Transylvania by force.

1774-1787 – Samuel von Brukenthal, counselor of Empress Maria Theresa, becomes governor of Transylvania.

1780-1790 – Joseph II attempts to impose enlightened reforms from the top down in the Habsburg Empire.

1835 – The General Savings House opens in Brasov.

1845 – The Transylvanian Saxon Agricultural Association is founded.

1848 – The revolution in Vienna reaches Transylvania. Romanians and Saxons remain on the side of the emperor; civil war ensues, and Reghin is torched.

1867 – The dual, Austrian-Hungarian state is formed; Transylvania is annexed to the Magyar half of the empire.

1872 – The first meeting of all Saxons in Transylvania is held in Medias.

1876 – Definitive annulment of the crown domain; new administrative land division.

1885 – Dr. Carl Wolff founds the first Raiffeisen-type consumer cooperative.

1918 – The Declaration of Alba Iulia: Transylvanian Romanians proclaim their unification with Romania.

1919 – The Union of Germans in Romania is founded.

1921 – The first agricultural reform in Transylvania.

1940 – Romania loses Bassarabia, Northern Bukovina and Northern Ardeal to the U.S.S.R. and Hungary.

1941 – Romania enters the war against U.S.S.R. on Germany's side.

1942-1943 – An agreement is established between Germany, Hungary and Romania on the enrollment of ethnic Germans in the Wehrmacht.

1944 (August 23rd) – Romania capitulates and declares war against its former allies.

September 6-19 1944 – Saxons are evacuated from Northern Ardeal.

1945 – German ethnics are deported to labor camps in the U.S.S.R. Their lands are expropriated as part of a second agricultural reform.

1947-June 1948 – The law for the nationalization of production capacities is passed. In August 1948, schools (even religious schools) are also nationalized – a hard blow for Saxon churches.

1949 – The Evangelical Church of Augustan Confession in Romania adopts its new Internal Regulations; the Union of Transylvanian Saxons Living in Germany is founded.

1950 – German ethnics in Romania regain their right to vote.

1951 – Many people from Banat, including about 10,000 Swabians, are sent to the Romanian Plain by forced evacuation.

1956 – German ethnics are given back their houses together with their new occupants. Saxons only have the right to live in one or two rooms of their homes.

1978 – An agreement is established between Chancellor Schmidt and Ceausescu for the emigration of ethnic Germans, with the purpose of reuniting families.

1981 – Deep economic crisis in Romania. Even bare necessities are very hard to come by.

1989 – Fall of the Ceausescu regime. Founding of the Democratic Forum of Germans in Romania.

1990-1992 – Mass emigration. Most Saxons return to the West.

1996 – The number of parishioners of the Evangelical Church of Augustan Confession in Romania is 17,867 (only two decades earlier, there were ten times as many).

ART&CREDITS

Preface: **Map of German Transylvania**, by Radu Oltean. Although there were several waves of immigration over more than two centuries, the colonization of Transylvania was a planned one. The colonists reached Hungary following the course of the Danube. Then they crossed the Tisa River. Those who went up the Mures River were settled on the royal lands, in southern Transylvania, on a strip between Orastie and Baraolt with its northern limit in the Tarnave area; those who went up the Somes River, ended up in the Bistrita area, where most of the Saxon villages would be subject to either the lay or the clerical nobility.

Part 1: **Building Sibiu.** by Radu Oltean. Saxons came, worked, and built in Transylvania a civilization that reached its peak in the 16th century.

Part 2 : **What was Sibiu like in the 17th century?** by Radu Oltean. Artist Radu Oltean's drawing shows the complete restoration of the stronghold and the surrounding lakes.

Part 3: **Annual market in Sibiu**, by Franz Neuhauser, Brukenthal National Museum. Franz Neuhauser depicted, after nature, the atmosphere of a late 18th century Transylvanian market, capturing types of residents of Sibiu in their characteristic costumes, distinguished according to social status, ethnicity and profession.

Part 4: **Biertan,** by Radu Oltean. In the heart of a traditional Saxon village, you are greeted from afar by the famous fortified church, Romania's first monument included in the UNESCO World Heritage list.

THE END

Thank you for reading my book. I hope you enjoyed it!

Would you do me a small favor?

I'd love to hear from you and what you thought of this book!

If you could take a few moments, click on the link below and write a blurb on Amazon about this book.

Your feedback will help others to learn about this book and help me learn how I can better serve my readers.

Click here to leave me a review on Amazon.com: http://www.amazon.com/dp/B00DV3WSVW

You can reach me at www.catalingruia.com or on Facebook

Like me on Facebook: www.facebook.com/ByCatalinGruia

Thank so much, I hope to hear from you and I wish you all the best!

Catalin

ABOUT THE AUTHOR

Catalin Gruia is a veteran journalist who has written and reported for the Romanian edition of National Geographic for over 10 years. He is currently Editor in Chief of National Geographic Traveler and Deputy Editor in Chief of National Geographic Romania.

INTERNATIONAL AWARDS

· **First prize (Geographica category)** at the International Seminar of National Geographic International Editions, Washington, 2004

· **Johann Strauss Golden Medal**, Vienna, 2010

· **Kinarri Trophy**, Friends of Thailand Awards, Bangkok, 2013

ACKNOWLEDGEMENTS

Thanks to my friends Dragos Margoi, Anca Barbulescu and Tudor Smalenic who encouraged me and helped make this project happen.

Also, special thanks to: Radu Oltean, Bogdan Croitoru, Madalina Nan, Pancras Dijk, Alina Alexa, Razvan Pascu, Adina Branciulescu, Roxana Farca, Klaus Birthler, Cezar Dumitru, Gabriela Cocea, Andreea Campeanu, Diana Tret, Anca Popescu and Brukenthal National Museum

ALSO BY CATALIN GRUIA

Romania Explained To My Friends Abroad

Why We Love Vienna

Thailand With A Baby Stroller

Printed in Great Britain
by Amazon